Introduction to

Dream

Interpretation

Dr. Juanita Woodson

Copyright © 2019 by Dr. Juanita Woodson

All rights reserved. This book or any portion thereof may not be reproduced or used in any manner whatsoever without the express written permission of the publisher except for the use of brief quotations in a book review.

Scriptures marked KJV are taken from the KING JAMES VERSION (KJV): KING JAMES VERSION, public domain. Unless otherwise stated.

Printed in the United States of America

First Printing, 2019

Impact Development Foundation Inc.

Impact Book Publishing

950 Eagles Landing Pkwy

Suite #924

Stockbridge GA, 30281

www.DrJuanitaWoodson.com

www.impact-development.org

Table of Contents

Introduction to Dream Interpretation 1

Chapter 1: What Are Dreams? 4

Chapter 2: How to Interpret Dreams God's Way 8

Chapter 3: 3 Main Sources of a Dream: God—You—Satan 13

Chapter 4: 5 Main Guidelines to Interpreting Dreams 18

Definitions, Symbols, and Explanations 22

About the Author 31

Introduction to Dream Interpretation

Since the age of five, I've experienced vivid and profound dreams. In the early days, many of my dreams revolved around hell and its fury. I often woke up crying, overwhelmed by the terrifying scenes I had witnessed. I remember flames, the agonized screams of souls, and the oppressive heat, like standing in a furnace. One recurring vision was of a large, menacing woman seated on a throne in what looked like a cavern filled with prison-like compartments. She radiated pure evil and controlled everything within that dark realm, directing people to their designated cells.

My dreams weren't confined to hell; they also foretold war, destruction, and even the return of Christ, including the rapture. Crowds of people running from danger, chaos, and disaster became a common theme. As I grew older, the tone of my dreams shifted. I began to see myself as an advocate, leading groups of people to safety. I somehow always knew the safest path to a haven and urged others to follow me. But not everyone would listen. Those who chose another direction often met destruction, despite my desperate pleas.

With time, my ability to interpret these dreams deepened, and their meaning became clearer. I saw myself creating a safe place for people fleeing destruction, even facing threats like dragons and disasters. In one dream, I stood boldly against a dragon, declaring he had no authority over the people I was protecting. Though he roared and tried to destroy me, I refused to bow or waver. When he realized he couldn't break me, he left defeated.

These dreams, though frightening, were uniquely crafted by God to reveal my calling and destiny. They unveiled my assignment: to rescue people from darkness and lead them into freedom. Not everyone is called to fight dragons or deliver others from danger, but this was my divine training ground, a personal encounter with God in my sleep.

Everyone dreams according to their purpose. What you're called to do and who you're meant to be will often manifest in your dreams. Growing up in a pastor's home, I was taught to fear the Lord and prepare for Christ's return. Weekly teachings on the rapture and warnings about hell shaped my early beliefs—and many of my dreams reflected those fears. Though hell is real, salvation eliminates the need for fear. Instead, our dreams often mirror the contents of our hearts, whether love, desires, or even fears. This is why discerning whether a dream is from God is crucial.

Dreams can stem from three sources: God, your soul, or the enemy. Dreams from your soul reflect your own desires and thoughts, which can sometimes be misaligned with God's will. Praying in this direction might lead you astray, as it reflects your will rather than His. On the other hand, dreams from the enemy exploit spiritual weaknesses, sowing discord, fear, and lies. The enemy's goal is to lead you away from God's purpose.

Understanding dreams requires spiritual discernment. I believe my early dreams held keys to my destiny, showing me that my calling is to pull people out of darkness and destruction, bringing them into deliverance and freedom. Through these dreams, God was preparing me for a mission uniquely tailored to my life and His kingdom.

Sincerely,

Dr. Juanita Woodson

CHAPTER 1

WHAT ARE DREAMS?

Chapter 1
What Are Dreams?

A dream is a succession of images, ideas, emotions, and sensations that usually occur involuntarily in the mind during certain stages of sleep. ... Dreams mainly occur in the rapid-eye movement (REM) stage of sleep—when brain activity is high and resembles that of being awake.

What are other types of dreams?

1. Day dream- a series of pleasant thoughts that distract one's attention from the present.
2. Lucid Dream-where you realize in the dream that you are dreaming and sometimes can control the outcomes.
3. Déjà vu- a feeling of having already experienced the present situation.
4. A tedious familiarity.
5. Recurrent Dreams- When you dream the same thing over and over
6. Nightmares- A nightmare is a disturbing dream that causes the dreamer to wake up feeling anxious and frightened.

Two Important key elements to dreams:

Imagination- the faculty or action of forming new ideas, or images or concepts of external objects not present to the senses. The ability of the mind to be creative or resourceful, the part of the mind that imagines things.

Fantasy- the activity of imagining desirable things, especially things that seem impossible or improbable.

Medical Studies & Claims

According to Medical News Today, these are the facts they found about dreams.

- Everyone dreams between 3 and 6 times per night.
- Each dream lasts between 5 to 20 minutes.
- Around 95 percent of dreams are forgotten by the time a person gets out of bed.
- Dreaming can help you learn and develop long-term memories.
- Blind people dream more with other sensory components compared with sighted people.

In conclusion, the Medical News Today says that scientist can't really explain why we dream, and they are unsure whether they have any meaning or relevancy.

However, we understand that dreams can be divinely inspired, carrying profound insight and revelation on various subjects, offering guidance for our future and the future of others.

Cultural Influence

Dreams will be usually Interpreted according to your personal and cultural perception of people, places, things:

- Cultural myths and superstition, including old wives' tales, passed down beliefs, notions, and legends are all ideals that shape your belief system and they are imbedded in your soul.
- <u>The definition of Superstition</u> is a widely held but unjustified belief in supernatural causation leading to certain consequences of an action or event, or a practice based on such a belief, (for ex. An itchy hand means money)
- How you feel about people, places, things and animals in reality is usually how you should interpret them in dreams unless they clearly appear differently
- For Ex: dogs- If you love dogs, every dog you dream about may not represent an enemy but rather a friend.
- God may be represented by a teacher, mentor, pastor or father figure you look up to in a dream.

As a believer God wants you to use His perspective and model of interpretation when giving you dreams.

CHAPTER 2

How to Interpret Dreams God's Way

CHAPTER 2
HOW TO INTERPRET DREAMS GOD'S WAY

The Bible contains over 2,550 references to dreams, each showcasing their significance in divine communication. The first mention appears in **Genesis 20:3-7**, where God speaks to Abimelech in a dream after he takes Abraham's wife, Sarah, intending to marry her. In the dream, God warns Abimelech not to touch her, threatening death if he disobeys. Instead, God instructs him to return Sarah to Abraham and seek his prayers.

In Genesis 28, God gives Jacob a powerful dream of angels ascending and descending a ladder—an image often referred to as "Jacob's Ladder." Later, in Genesis 31, Jacob's father-in-law, Laban, receives a dream from God, warning him to be cautious about how he speaks to Jacob.

Perhaps the most well-known dreamer in the Bible is Joseph, introduced in Genesis 37. Joseph, the next-to-youngest son of Jacob, has prophetic dreams that reveal his destiny and set the stage for his extraordinary journey. These moments highlight how God uses dreams to guide, warn, and reveal His plans to individuals.

Genesis 37:6-11 (ASV)

⁶ And he said unto them, Hear, I pray you, this dream which I have dreamed:

⁷ for, behold, we were binding sheaves in the field, and, lo, my sheaf arose, and also stood upright; and, behold, your sheaves came round about, and made obeisance to my sheaf.

⁸ And his brethren said to him, Shalt thou indeed reign over us? Or shalt thou indeed have dominion over us? And they hated him yet the more for his dreams, and for his words.

⁹ And he dreamed yet another dream, and told it to his brethren, and said, Behold, I have dreamed yet a dream: and, behold, the sun and the moon and eleven stars made obeisance to me.

¹⁰ And he told it to his father, and to his brethren; and his father rebuked him, and said unto him, What is this dream that thou hast dreamed? Shall I and thy mother and thy brethren indeed come to bow down ourselves to thee to the earth?

¹¹ And his brethren envied him; but his father kept the saying in mind.

What's important to understand in this passage of scripture is that everyone except Joesph could interpret his dream. Joseph was obviously new to dreams at this point and if he only knew the interpretation he may have kept it to himself. In the end, Joseph's dream comes to past. He eventually learns how to interpret dreams and not only is his life changed forever but the lives of his entire family.

Genesis 40:8 (ASV)

⁸ And they said unto him, We have dreamed a dream, and there is none that can interpret it. And Joseph said unto them, Do not interpretations belong to God? tell it me, I pray you.

Genesis 41:15-16 (ASV)

¹⁵ And Pharaoh said unto Joseph, I have dreamed a dream, and there is none that can interpret it: and I have heard say of thee, that when thou hearest a dream thou canst interpret it.

¹⁶ And Joseph answered Pharaoh, saying, It is not in me: God will give Pharaoh an answer of peace.

Joseph's interpretation of Pharaoh's dream led to his remarkable promotion to second-in-command, ruling over all the land of Egypt. During the severe famine that Joseph had foretold, his father and brothers came seeking mercy, fulfilling the earlier dreams Joseph had shared with them.

In our time, God has promised to pour out His Spirit on all flesh, and this includes the gift of dreams. This prophecy, first spoken by the prophet Joel, was confirmed by the Apostle Peter on the Day of Pentecost. As Peter preached, he referenced Joel 2:28, declaring that in the last days, God's Spirit would inspire visions, dreams, and prophetic insight in people of all ages and backgrounds.

Joel 2:28 (ASV)

[28] And it shall come to pass afterward, that I will pour out my Spirit upon all flesh; and your sons and your daughters shall prophesy, your old men shall dream dreams, your young men shall see visions:

God gives dreams for a purpose and we must take time to learn how to interpret them properly.

Chapter 3

3 Main Sources of a Dream: God—You—Satan

Chapter 3

3 Main Sources of a Dream: God—You—Satan

Dreams can originate from three primary sources, and understanding these sources is crucial for interpreting their meaning and purpose. Each source serves a distinct role:

1. **God**: Dreams from God often reveal His plans, purposes, and love. They may serve as warnings, provide direction or instruction, or offer a glimpse into your future. These dreams can also bring healing from past pain or prepare you for significant life events such as the birth of a child, a wedding, or even a loss. God's dreams are designed to guide, comfort, and align you with His will.

2. **You (Self)**: Dreams stemming from yourself reflect the inner workings of your heart and mind. They may highlight your fears, insecurities, desires, imagination, or even memories. Factors like what you ate before bed or a movie you recently watched can also influence these dreams. These are typically personal and emotionally driven.

3. **Satan**: The enemy uses dreams to disrupt God's purpose in your life. Such dreams may encourage selfishness, promote fear, doubt, and distrust in God or loved ones, or sow discord and sin. They can introduce vain imaginations, temptations, and confusion, sometimes even masquerading as God's will by appealing to your deepest desires. These dreams are designed to torment and mislead, often creating spiritual or emotional turmoil.

Recognizing the source of your dreams allows you to respond appropriately and align yourself with God's truth and purpose.

Dreams from God come for several reasons:

Dreams from God serve a variety of profound purposes, each designed to guide, encourage, and prepare you. These divine messages carry prophetic significance, encompassing wisdom, knowledge, and understanding. Here are the key reasons why God gives dreams:

- To encourage, warn and prepare
- To show you what to pray for and who to pray for
- To show what He's going to do in the future
- To direct you, instruct you, and reveal things you cannot see

Every dream that comes from God will have a prophetic purpose and will include (wisdom, knowledge, and understanding).

Remember that Prophesy speaks to the past, the present, & the future of an individual.

1. He wants to heal or reveal something from your past to help you understand what you need to be healed from, change or to understand so you can move forward to a better life.
   - Generational curses and cycles that need to be broken
   - To pinpoint when a particular event happened that caused your set back
   - The death of a love one
   - Divorce, -ejection, that caused
   - Low self-esteem, low self-worth
   - Doubt, fear to enter
   - Reminder of prophecy that God is still going to honor
   - Reminder of something important you need to remember
2. He wants to help you with your present life by revealing things that you haven't noticed or simply don't know, and to share keys that can help you advance in many areas. For example:
   - Who current enemies are
   - What job to take
   - Which church to attend
   - Who to connect with and who to disconnect from
   - What your kids are up to
   - What the enemy has planned

- What decisions to make
- Who to pray for
- What traps or plots lay in wait for you

3. He wants to prepare and encourage you for your future by revealing things that can help you:
    - Preparation for the death of a loved one
    - Preparation for a physical move locally, nationally or internationally
    - Prepare you for a job promotion or new business
    - Prepare you for an upcoming test or trial
    - Prepare you for a divine visitation from Him
    - Prepare you for any hardship on the horizon
    - Prepare for a birth or a wedding

CHAPTER 4

5 Main Guidelines to Interpreting Dreams

Chapter 4
5 Main Guidelines to Interpreting Dreams

Settings are very important in a dream. It will determine whether the dream is literal, spiritual or metaphoric in nature. Understanding how you feel in a dream also helps you determine how you will feel in reality.

1. What was the Setting? Where did the dream takes place? What was the scenery?
    - House, car, school, jail, hospital, church
    - City and state, country
    - Outside, field, mountain top, trees, ocean, lakes etc.
2. What's happening? What is going on in the dream?
    - Are you watching it happen?
    - Are you participating?
    - Is it a storm, fire, flood, murder, fight, robbery, war, funeral, church service?
    - Were wild animals or reptiles chasing you
    - Did you see angels, were you flying, etc.

3. How you feel in the dream? -What were your emotions like?
    - Did you laugh?
    - Did you cry?
    - Were you afraid or scared?
    - Were you excited?
    - Were you hopeful or hopeless?
    - Were you let down or shocked?
4. How do you feel when you wake up? Did the dream feel real upon waking? What other emotions did you notice after waking?
    - Were you crying
    - Laughing
    - Fearful
    - Hopeful
    - Feel betrayed
    - Numb
    - Did you feel like you were really there
    - Did you bring anything out the dream with you (for example were you still clutching a key now invisible that someone gave you in the dream)
    - Were you physically sore after waking up from a dream of a fight or
    - Battle?

5. What does the word of God say about anything that sticks out to you in the dream? For example: did anything resemble these scriptures?
    - Jeremiah 29:11- God's Plans are good and not evil to bring you to an expected end. So God wants to bless and not curse.
    - Deuteronomy 28:1-14- Says you will be blessed in every area of your life if you Obey God
    - Isaiah 61:1-9 Speaks of how Christ was anointed specifically to break yokes of bondage, heal the broken hearted, give beauty for ashes, give joy instead of mourning, give double for trouble, to relieve heaviness
    - John 10:10- takes about the thief coming to still kill and destroy
    - 1 Peter 5:8 speaks of the devil going to and fro like a roaring lion seeking whom he may devour

Definitions, Symbols, and Explanations

Definitions, Symbols, and Explanations

Death—birds flying through house, or sitting in windows; crows; people dying or being killed that seem real and extremely sad; dream someone reveals they are dying; funerals, people with wings, someone sick or disabled becomes suddenly whole (in the dream) etc. (could be spiritual or natural)

Birth-- (pregnancy) dreams of- eating fish, seafood, crab legs, shrimp; labor and delivery room; mid wife; OBGYN doctor; pregnant belly, birthing; birthing gifts, new ideas, a ministry, etc. (could all be spiritual or natural)

Money—(losing it or gaining it), purse, wallet, dollars, coins, lottery, etc (could all be spiritual or natural)

Moving—relocating, transferring, Uhaul, trailers, new home, new city, house actually moving as a vehicle, etc (could all be spiritual or natural)

Animals—

Bird-Birds-doves (Holy Spirit) or dead in Christ, crows are evil and used in witchcraft, buzzards are for death and dead things etc. Parrots are beautiful spirited people.

Elephant-life companion, danger, destruction, memories, idols

Bulls- idolatry, idols, stubborn, or farm animals, an attack

Horse- power, speed, ride, (depends on what horse is doing)

Lion- (if fearful- satan), promiscuity, sexual sin, if godly it could be Christ Jesus, an attack on the way, etc.

Tiger- stripes could represent markers for trouble. Spiritual attack, lust promiscuity. Bears-bold demons, pushy people, spiritual attack, powerful force

Reptiles— enemy; (wicked people), deadly, destruction, satanic, attack, witchcraft.

Snakes- demonic; Python, Venomous Snakes, Non-venomous lizards, alligator, crocodile, frogs, witchcraft, spells, hex, witch in disguise, (could be natural or spiritual)

Insects—demonic, unclean, ungodly, witchcraft, (natural and spiritual)

Spiders, bugs, roaches, caterpillar, ants, fly, grasshopper, moth- evil and unclean spirits, demonic infestation.

Natural Disaster—(hurricane, tornado, flood, earthquake, rain, snow, hail, Lightening etc) life calamity, destruction, uprooting, breaking of stubborn wills, removal of people and things, clearing out of the old preparing for the new, major change or shift

House—(windows, doors, office, kitchen, living room, basement, attic etc) you, your soulish realm, your thoughts, emotions, understanding, learning, a church, the past, your family history, generational curses and issues

Locations--New York, Chicago, Paris, China, Dubai, Africa (literal or spiritual implications of an event)

Colors-

Red-- The Blood of Jesus, sacrifice, seduction, war, battle, the tabernacle

Blue—Royalty, priesthood, freedom, redemption, salvation

Gold—Godly, heaven, kingly, wealth, riches

Yellow—Sunshine, new day, warmth, joy, hope, grace

Green—new growth, wealth, birth, blessings, new beginning

White—purification, forgiven sins, sanctification, baptism, cleansing, washing, also could be hypocrites, liars, false pretenders

Black— empty slate for creation, place of faith, trusting God in the dark, or place of ignorance, darkness, evil,

Purple—Royalty, wealth, kingly, high rank official

Police—(jail, prison, dungeon, court, warrant, arrest, officer, cell mate) could be literal or spiritual, demonic accusation, demonic attacks, belief in untruths, owing a debt, generational curses blocking, religion, pride, bondage, being arrested by God to do His will, un-forgiveness etc.

Numbers and Sequences (best when used with the Bible)

1—Unity, oneness of God, sovereignty of God, absolute, ultimate power, highest rank, best choice, second to none

2—Covenant, agreement, bond, marriage, tie

3—Three in one God, unbreakable three cord strand, completion

4—Supernatural, our seasons, four directions; north, south, east and west, for corners of the earth, spirit realm

5—Grace, mercy, help, kindness, favor of God

6—Man, human race, tripled is satan and mark of the beast, flesh, sin nature of man

7—Perfection, completion, rest, accomplishment,

8—New beginning, fresh start, reset

9—Fruit, Fruitfulness (nine fruits of the Holy Spirit), grace, spiritual completion, supplication completion, full term pregnancy, month of the spiritual new year

10—Tithe, judgement, God's law, reward whether good or bad

11—Walking in agreement, nearing the end of a season, falling short, missing the mark, confusion, the anti-christ

12—Government, governing systems both natural and spiritual, legal transactions, apostolic, authoritative,

Family--(sisters, brothers, mother, father, cousins, aunt, uncle, grandparents, children), generational curses, family secrets, abuse, inheritance, the church, saved individuals, etc; all can be taken literal or spiritual

Church—(pastors, preacher, church building, children, school bus, sharks, sheep, wolves etc) can be good or bad, usually means a literal church, spiritually the Body of Christ, wolves and sharks are pastors that prey on the flock

Body Parts-

Arms—strength, power, God's upholding (with His right arm), might; (shoulder) to lean on, compassion as in giving or receiving hugs.

Hands—helping, giving, supporting, mercy, grace, available for God's use; if dirty could mean sin, defiled, unclean, unable to please God; blood on hands could mean one being at fault for someone else's downfall or demise; if hands are bitten, chopped off, hurt it could mean someone you helped either used you deceitfully, despised your help, and or you or took it for granted.

Feet--your direction, your belief, your stance, your rooting and grounding; gym shoes could represent running from a calling; bare feet could symbolize holy ground (as in the presence of God); one who preaches the gospel; could be literally interpreted for health concerns; cut off feet could mean detachment from mobility; diseased feet represent spiritual issues and improper armor (as in feet shod with the preparation of the gospel of peace).

Head—Your mind, thoughts, will, the top, the leader, place of salvation, thoughts, ideas, faith, imagination, place of decision making, must allow God to control.

Genitals or Nakedness-- things hidden being revealed usually embarrassing (as in buttocks or female breasts), shocking, uncovering of sin, open shame, full nakedness could mean death (as in naked I came into the world and naked I will leave this world), could mean bareness in women or impotence in males. (Spiritually or naturally);partial nakedness could mean partial revealing of a deeper situation.

Hair—A woman's glory or sense of beauty, strength (as in Samson) literally or spiritually, could mean witchcraft if used in food, used to make spells, or if seen eating (denotes exposure to false teaching).

Tongue—Ones tongue literally or spiritually; words spoken of good or evil, life or death, word curses; or words of blessings; if used by an animal like a lion or tiger licking could mean destruction or becoming the enemy's prey.

Eyes—Spiritual or literal; seeing into the spirit realm; prophetic understanding and wisdom, supernatural insight, faith; doubt if eyes are cloudy; spiritually blind; if seen as a third eye considered witchcraft and access to the occult realm.

Nose—Spiritual discernment, prayer, intercession, good or evil presence detection; fragrance either spiritual or natural of sin, illness, rain (blessings), rose of Sharon (Jesus).

Heart—After God's heart; soul-ish desires; Godly desires; wicked desires; either purified or tainted, can be literal or spiritual; natural heart as in health concerns; A place your treasure lies (as in personal money received or earned)

Transportation Vehicles:

Includes one's (life, goals, family, ministry, career, school, marriage, purpose, ideas etc); expresses speed, levels of growth, fast or slow. Can mean promotion to higher levels and also demotions to lower levels of progress. If there's an accident or damage to the vehicle it can be a warning of danger to come or that has already happened. Can be literal or spiritual depending on aspects talked about earlier in this book.

Airplane- speed(faster than a car or train), airborne, higher realms, heavenly connection, usually a good indication of spiritual growth unless naturally discerned; (can be spiritual or natural); accidents or crashes may mean avoid making bad decisions.

Train- (faster than a car, slower than an airplane) moving, travel, symbolic of holidays or past memories involving trains, slower but steady progression in a direction whether good or bad; train crashes are caused by bad decisions (could result in literal crash or spiritual backsliding)

Jet-(extremely fast pace), airborne, out of reach, (could be spiritual or natural, positive or negative); will reach destination usually in less the time then an airplane; going higher in the things(understanding, wisdom, knowledge, gifts) of God;

redeeming loss time; becoming wealthy quickly (power to get wealth and riches). Out of the enemy's grasp.

Car- moving along at the ground level; could mean consistency, earth realm or in the supernatural realm, fast cars (ie. sports cars) represent accelerated speed on a lower or advanced level.

Van-Family, family/small business, lineage, bloodline, multi passengers going in the same direction together

Boat-salvation; a means to navigate the soul's emotions, especially with confusion; (as in sea of emotions), could represent safety from drowning in sin; safety from harm and danger; could also mean rebellion when interpreted as a Jonah.

School bus- Can mean literal school or school bus; a church (as in carrying children of God), pastoral calling, being a pastor; starting or founding a school on any grade level; specific programs; educational transport or vehicle to educational institutions (as in helping someone with admissions), levels of spiritual or natural understanding (K-12 vs college levels) and growth.

About the Author

Dr. Juanita Woodson is an apostle of Jesus Christ, anointed with several gifts of the Holy Spirit. Known for her renowned prophetic voice, she carries a profound passion for evangelism, healing and deliverance. Dr. Woodson believes wholeheartedly in the life-transforming power of prayer and prophecy, and her ministry is marked by  miracles, signs, wonders, and testimonies of breakthrough and deliverance from believers worldwide.

With over two decades of experience in ministry, Dr. Woodson has traveled extensively, fortifying and building ministries across the nations. She leads ministry cohorts, equipping leaders in the five-fold ministry and deliverance. Her heart is in empowering leaders within the Body of Christ, ensuring they are well-equipped to set captives free and lead with boldness and integrity.

As a wife, and mother, Dr. Woodson has gracefully navigated the many roles she fulfills. In addition to her apostolic work, she is an author, counselor, wealth coach, and sought-after public speaker. Together with her husband, they are serial entrepreneurs, focused on building generational legacies.. Dr. Woodson serves as the CEO of a nonprofit organization called Impact Development Foundation that provides basic needs assistance, education, counseling, and advocacy to families in need. She empowers men and women to RECOVER and BREAK FREE from chains of poverty, depression, financial setbacks, and failure..

Dr. Woodson's journey to success was not without challenges. Having faced financial hardship, including eviction, repossession, and bankruptcy, she is intimately familiar with the struggle to rise above. Despite being labeled with a learning disability in her youth, Dr. Woodson earned four degrees (2 BA, 1 MA, 1 D.Min) in Psychology and Christian Counseling with highest honors, and currently attends Princeton Theological Seminary.

Grateful for the opportunity to impact lives, Dr. Woodson gives all glory to God for every success and lesson learned. She remains committed to advancing the Kingdom of God, equipping leaders, and raising up entrepreneurs, determined to leave a lasting legacy of faith, empowerment, and freedom.

God Bless you! Sincerely,
Dr. Juanita Woodson
www.drjuanitawoodson.com
Impact Development Foundation
impact-development.org